A PRIMER about the FLAG

Marvin Bell

illustrated by **Chris Raschka**

CANDLEWICK PRESS

Or certain ones.

There are Bed & Breakfast flags.

They fly over vacancies,

but seldom above full houses.

Shipboard, the bridge can say

an alphabet of flags.

There are   State flags

and
State Fair
flags,

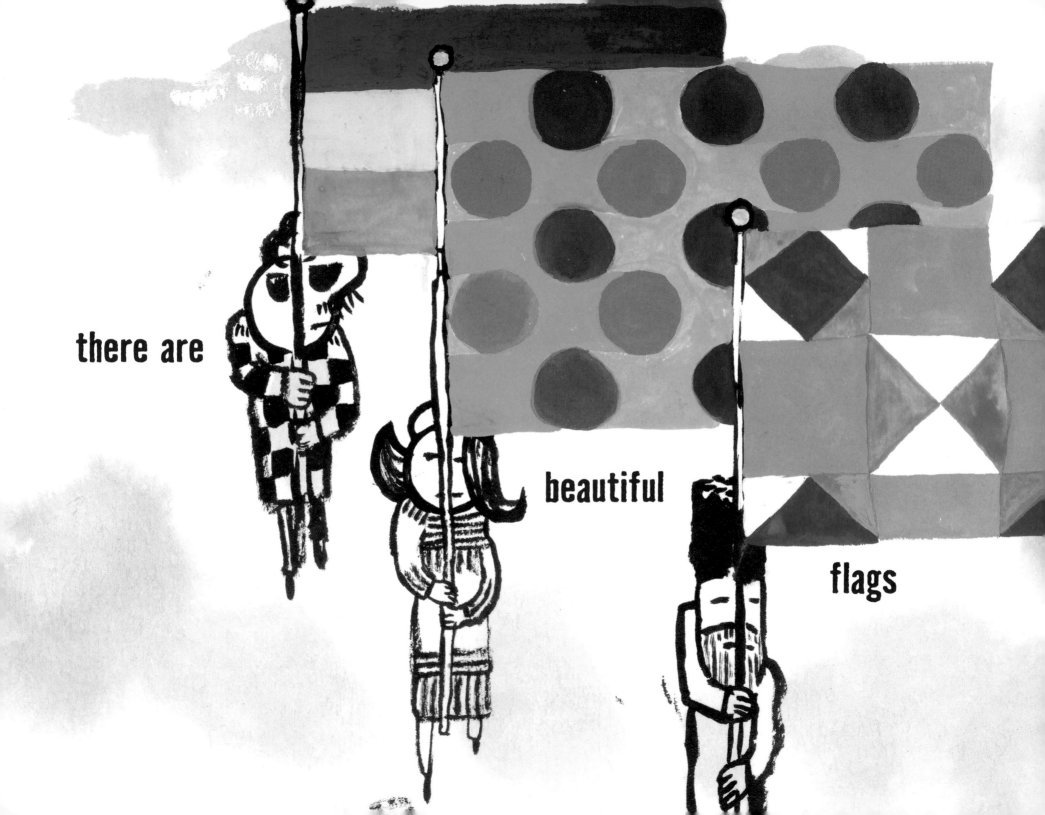

and enemy flags.

Enemy flags are not supposed to be

or long-lasting.

There are flags on the moon, flags in cemeteries,

costume flags.

There are little flags that come from the barrel

and say,

If you want to have

a parade,

you usually have to have a flag

for people to line up behind.

Few would line up behind a small tree, for example,

if you carried it at your waist just like a flag

but didn't first tell people what it stood for.

A Primer about the Flag

Or certain ones. There are Bed & Breakfast flags.
They fly over vacancies, but seldom
above full houses. Shipboard, the bridge can say
an alphabet of flags. There are State flags
and State Fair flags, there are beautiful flags
and enemy flags. Enemy flags are not supposed
to be beautiful, or long-lasting. There are flags
on the moon, flags in cemeteries, costume flags.
There are little flags that come from the barrel
of a gun and say, "Bang." If you want to have
a parade, you usually have to have a flag
for people to line up behind. Few would
line up behind a small tree, for example,
if you carried it at your waist just like a flag
but didn't first tell people what it stood for.

To Colman and Aileen
M. B.

For Paul
C. R.

Text copyright © 2011 by Marvin Bell. Published by arrangement with Copper Canyon Press. Illustrations copyright © 2011 by Chris Raschka. All rights reserved. No part of this book may be reproduced, transmitted, or stored in an information retrieval system in any form or by any means, graphic, electronic, or mechanical, including photocopying, taping, and recording, without prior written permission from the publisher. First edition 2011. Library of Congress Cataloging-in-Publication Data is available. Library of Congress Catalog Card Number 2010038924. ISBN 978-0-7636-4991-3. Printed in Humen, Dongguan, China. This book was typeset in Badhouse. The illustrations were done in gouache and ink. Candlewick Press, 99 Dover Street, Somerville, Massachusetts 02144. visit us at www.candlewick.com
10 11 12 13 14 15 16 SCP 10 9 8 7 6 5 4 3 2 1